AMERICAN DREAMER

A Tale of Hope and New Beginnings

A Brief and Swift Guide to Thriving in America

CHOYO GOMEX

Disclaimer Notice:

Please note that the information contained within this document
for educational and entertainment purposes only. All effort ha
been executed to present accurate, up-to-date, reliable, ar
complete information. No warranties of any kind are declared
implied. Readers acknowledge that the author is not engaged
rendering legal, financial, medical, or professional advice. Th
content within this book has been derived from various source
Please consult a licensed professional before attempting an
techniques outlined in this book.

By reading this document, the reader agrees that the author
under no circumstances responsible for any direct or indire
losses incurred because of the use of the information containe
within this document, including, but not limited to, error
omissions, or inaccuracies.

Table of Contents

Introduction

Fellow Traveler,

My name is Choyo Gomex, and I'm not just the author of th
book—I am you.

I am the embodiment of dreams, resilience, and th
unwavering spirit that has brought countless immigrants like yc
and me to the shores of the United States.

Like you, I left my homeland, Mexico, in search of a bette
life, and I understand the hurdles, heartaches, blood, sweat, an
tears accompanying such a journey.

My journey was not on gold-plated pavement, and it was nc
without its hardships. I faced challenges that many of you kno\
all too well. I was deported from the United States not once, nc
twice, but six times. So, the frustration, the fear, the anger, and th
disappointment that come with deportation are emotions I'v
experienced firsthand. I've walked your path, faced simila
hurdles, and found a way to thrive in this remarkable nation.
share my story with you not to boast about my achievements bu
to assure and challenge you that if I could do it, it is within you
reach, too. If I rose above these challenges, why shouldn't you
The United States is a land of opportunities. Success in this lan
is not reserved for a select few, but it is not free; nothing is really

Success has its price, like everything else in life. If you want badly enough, you most certainly can obtain it if you're willing to do certain things in a certain way, work hard, persevere, and never give up. That is the price I found I had to pay to succeed in America.

I wrote this book because I know the importance of helping immigrants succeed in the United States, and I've been where you are now. It is my passion and desire to empower you to thrive in America. I've met countless others on this path and seen their struggles, aspirations, and potential. We, the immigrants to the United States, are the lifeblood of this nation. We bring with us diverse experiences, talents, and dreams that enrich the fabric of American society.

This book is more than just a guide. It's a testament to the strength of the human spirit. It's a hand reaching out to you, offering guidance, hope, and a sense of belonging in this vast and sometimes daunting country.

I hope that you will find the information and inspiration you need to navigate the complexities of the American dream through these pages.

In the chapters that follow, we'll explore practical steps succeed in the United States, from understanding the immigrati system to building a thriving career and much more. While I do endorse or encourage undocumented status, I recognize the ne for guidance in navigating the challenges that some of tho immigrants face as well.

This book is an invitation to dream big, work hard, persever and never surrender. It's a testament to the boundless possibiliti that await you in this great nation. As you read on, I encoura you to keep an open heart and an open mind. The United States a land of infinite possibilities, and I believe we can make yo dreams come true together.

Welcome to the journey of thriving in America. Togethe we'll embrace the challenges, seize the opportunities, and write story of success that will inspire generations to come. With war regards and unwavering faith from your fellow traveler,

Choyo Gomex

Chapter 1

Chapter 1

One of Millions

Choyo Gomex left his hometown in Mexico at the age of 1 in pursuit of the American dream. He was then a young man, an life in Mexico was not a bed of roses, to quote Cuauhtémoc, th last Mexican emperor and the name of one of Choyo's sons. Th author hoped America would offer a new beginning, th opportunity for a new and better life.

"El Norte," as America was referred to back then, was see as the embodiment of opportunities and fresh starts—the fountai of life itself.

Choyo's childhood was interesting, to say the least. Hi mother had eleven children, of whom only four survived. Can yo imagine? The odds of survival were around 44%. One nigh Choyo was awakened by his worried mother because a scorpio stung his 2-year-old brother; a Scorpion sting there wa considered deadly, and it turned out it was, as Choyo's brother di not survive. After an all-night battle, his mother was on her knee praying and begging God not to take his little boy. At around 1 am, the baby died; it was an unforgettable experience to this day.

To feed them, their mother will assure them that for every rolled tortilla with a glass of water, they'll take a soul out of purgatory, then ask them how many souls they have saved so far. They'll say five or six, and she'll respond, no mijo, there are thousands. You got to do better than that, so we went ahead with another tortilla with a glass of water, and soon, they were no longer hungry.

At a very young age, he started asking why. Why did some people have while most did not? And why was he one of the have-nots?

Ever since he could remember, he had questioned his position in life. He wanted to understand; he had to find out why some had while most didn't. Why? That question tortured his young mind constantly.

His decision to come north to America soon became an obsession. Being a minor, he could not leave his village without his mother's permission. He counted the days until he was 18 years old. A few days after his 18th birthday, he finally started the journey to El Norte that would forever change his life. His mother could no longer hold him, so against her will, she saw him pack his bag and head north.

After a long and tiring three-day bus ride, he arrived Tijuana, the U.S.-Mexico border.

In Tijuana, the first thing to do was to find a "coyote," smuggler, as they're called. That was not a problem because the hung out at the bus depot waiting for prey, for travelers wh wanted to cross the border illegally into the United States. As soc as he got off the bus, he was quickly approached by a couple c coyotes, and he chose the one that looked older and mor trustworthy—not a very scientific way to measure people, but th best he could do under the circumstances.

Now, his dream of getting to America was finally withi reach. He had a plan and was finally close to El Norte.

The coyote took him and a dozen other "pollos," as th "coyotes" called their prey, to his house.

When they got to the coyotes' house, they found that anothe group of people was already there. The other group had tried anc failed to cross the border the night before, and the coyote told them they would all try again tonight.

Sure enough, at 10 p.m., they started their midnight journey
o America. There were two groups of 25, each with its own
yote guide.

After walking the hills of Tijuana, the coyotes took them to
 opening in the barbed-wire fence at the border and crawled
der it into America. They walked through the hills for a while.
ter a couple of hours walking, they finally spotted a parked car
iting for them; it was a Ford Gran Torino, a big car that could
ke all 25 of them. Because Choyo was one of the smallest and
htest, he was put into the trunk of the car with four other people.

A feeling of panic arose as the trunk door slammed shut,
osing in the five pollos. The trunk stank and the dust created by
e tires on the dirt road made breathing almost impossible at the
ginning, but the desire to make it to America was greater than
e fear of dying. He was willing to die in his attempt to make it
 the promised land.

Luckily for him and the rest of the passengers, the car
ddenly stopped a few minutes later. They heard mumbles
tside the car. The mumbles turned into voices in English, and
e voices got louder. The pollos all held their breath as footsteps
proached the trunk. It was the border patrol officers; they had
en found again.

When the officers opened the trunk of the car, they cou
breathe fresh air. As relieved as they were, they were equal
saddened and disappointed because they would be returned
Mexico and have to try again the next night.

That was Choyo Gomex's first attempt to get into Americ
It turned out to be one of many. The same procedure was repeat
five more times until finally, one day, the car kept on going ar
going while all the passengers were praying with all their migl
inside the trunk, they were all praying to all known saints ar
probably even made up some of their own. They figured an ang
must be up there looking out for pollos.

The car kept going on the dirt road for a while longer. By the
after a few tries, it felt easier to breathe. I guess we had gotten use
to the smell of dirt and sticky feet. Suddenly, it felt like the c
was flying. They had reached a paved road, and the ride was s
smooth now—it felt great. A few hours later, they were in L
Angeles.

Choyo remembers getting out of the car and kissing th
ground. He was finally in America, in Los Angeles, Californi
A childhood dream was finally a reality.

Arriving in LA was just the beginning for Choyo—and for the millions of other immigrants who have similar stories.

Immigrants who have left their native countries to pursue the American dream share many experiences. They came here with empty pockets, hearts full of dreams, and a burning desire to succeed, to achieve. It did not matter that they were leaving their native countries for a foreign land that they knew nothing about, apart from the common notion of America as the land of opportunities. They knew America as the land of the free and home of the brave, where the only thing that may stop you is yourself and your unwillingness to pursue your dreams, and that was not going to happen to Choyo Gomex.

Do Won Chang

Another immigrant who left everything behind and came to America to start a new life is Do Won Chang. Born in South Korea on March 20, 1954, Do Won Chang moved to the United States in 1981 with his young wife. With only a small amount of money, Chang had to juggle three jobs to sustain his family. At the same time, he managed to start a savings fund.

At one point, Chang noticed that most of the customers he handled at his job at a gas station were extremely rich members of the fashion and luxury industry. This observation drove Chang to use the money in his savings fund to start a clothing store. By 1984, after just three years in America, Do Won Chang had a clothing store in the Highland Park neighborhood of Los Angeles. Eventually, the company blossomed and became a fashion powerhouse now known to the world as Forever 21 (*10 inspiring stories*, 2023).

ie beauty of the story of Do Won Chang is not just about
:rsonal virtues like self-determination, business acumen, or
telligence. This story is about a unique interconnection with
ith in the American dream—a man and a woman left their home
untry in pursuit of a dream they had only heard about from other
:ople. They had faith in themselves to make it. They identified
ith the ideals of the American dream, and the dream made way
r them. Their sacrifices, hard work, passion, and love for
isiness eventually gave birth to an empire.

Indra Nooyi

The American story is incomplete without the success stories of the nation's immigrants. Another such other story is that of Indra Nooyi. Born in Tamil Nadu, India, Indira Nooyi moved to the United States of America to pursue her postgraduate education at the prestigious Yale School of Management. She graduated from Yale with a master's degree in private and public management. Nooyi's magnificent academic record and work resume did not escape the attention of high-end CEOs who wanted her to be a part of their companies and organizations. By 1994, Nooyi found herself being a part of PepsiCo, where she kept an excellent track record. In 2001, Nooyi was named president and CEO of PepsiCo. After this, she maintained a consistent appearance in Forbes' top 100 most powerful women. In 2018, Indira Nooyi was named among the world's best CEOs (*1 inspiring stories*, 2023).

Indira Nooyi's story is another propelled by the ethos of the American dream, a woman who left her country with nothing but an excellent academic record and the hope that just maybe in that big, diverse land of America, there will be opportunities for her, too. America did not disappoint her. She did indeed reap the fruits of her labor. She was able to access the opportunities, and she was recognized for her hard work and excellence. Her background did not matter. Her excellent academic and work resume did. If they could do it.

You Can Do It, Too

The essence of this book is to showcase the beauty of t[h]
American dream and what those who believe in it have achieve[d]
In addition, it serves as a manual for those who now believe in t[h]
American dream as immigrants and want a fair share of t[h]
success story. The main reason for writing this book, besid[es]
providing an immigrant's manual to survival, is to let you kno[w]
that others have been through what you are going through. It [is]
here to remind you that you are not alone; many others have bee[n]
there and conquered. You are the representation of the immigra[nt]
spirit and the foundational stone in the collective immigrant stor[y]
Wanting to be successful in a land where opportunities are widel[y]
available for everyone who desires to grab them is no wil[d]
concept. Merit matters and is rewarded. Most immigrants wi[ll]
succeed in this land, and this book will show you how.

Chapter 2

Chapter 2

Understanding the American Culture and Society

American culture is uniquely individualistic. Individualism is impactful on the overall diversity and multiculturalism of American society. The essence of America's individualistic culture is to build up and protect the diversity of the American people. Before you exist as a race or a group, you exist and identify as an individual separate from the dictates of race or community. You exist as a person with dreams, hope, and ambition. You have the desire to go for your dreams come hell or high water. You see our dreams and ambitions make us. The American dream makes America.

America as a country has been built through pain and sorrow. Her people have endured insurmountable amounts of adversity. The American culture and society at large appreciate people for who they are. The construct of the American society ensures that vices like classism, racism, and ageism do not take the lead in shaping the present or the future of the society.

Culture is a complex collection of individual personalities, making it all beautiful and exciting—that everyone exists as their own person, away from familial, racial, or professional collective existence.

Ultimately, individual personalities shape the overall outlook of the American culture, society, and social construct as it is. The very essence of culture is that it trains every individual to do better on their own, to shape themselves without relying on the general society to shape them. Ultimately, the shaping of self becomes a collective shaping of the American culture and society.

American society completely contrasts with societies in countries where most people come from the same place and share common blood. For instance, Indian society is based on joint family units, and as such, individualism is minimal.

The same applies to most African communities, where many people have blood ties. In countries like Kenya, a whole village might share a common ancestor, which is almost impossible in an American society because your neighbors are of diverse descent.

American Values, Norms, and Social Etiquette

Some of the values and norms of the American culture ar
individualism, equality, directness, informality, and observance
time (*U.S. culture*, n.d.). On the aspect of individualism, yo
identity—who you identify as and who you want to be—
paramount. Society is not going to tell you who you are. It is o
you to tell society who you are or, better still, showcase who yo
are. You will be viewed as an individual, not as your race or yo
family.

Equality is the foundational ethos of the American culture a
we know it today. Equality in this context means access t
opportunities equally and fairly, without discrimination.

In a way, it is the aspect of equality that shapes ho
everything else happens in American society. It shapes the cultur
in ways that no other aspects could. It has put the American cultur
on a trajectory where everyone matters. Opportunities ar
accessible on a merit basis as opposed to racial or classis
standards. Essentially, it does not matter who you are, where yo
come from, or your parents. Success is open for all in America.

Directness is one of the most critical aspects of the American way of life. Almost everyone approaches their issues or other people with a certain directness. Americans do not beat around the bush. If something is wrong, someone will point it out with fierce and non-contradictory directness, which is just the American way.

When I say informality, I mean, for instance, how successful people who, despite tremendous achievements, have a knack for humble appearances even though they could have big money; this can be seen in the often casual and straightforward dress code. Even the founder and CEO of Facebook, Mark Zuckerberg, has been known for his humble, casual appearance. Despite the tremendous success, American rapper and musician Jermaine Cole is often seen around riding a bicycle and clad in Crocs. The aim is to dress for comfort and not for rules.

The observance of time—or punctuality—is also incorporated into the American way of life. Efficiency is a societal as well as a cultural expectation. There is always the need to be time-conscious. Efficiency begins with the observance of time in the fulfillment of whatever task there may be. Most Americans expect you to be at work early and keep your appointments on time.

Discussion on Cultural Diversity and Tolerance

Cultural diversity is the bedrock of the American story as we know it and it sets America up for a more fantastic and better future as envisioned. It is the existence of different cultures in the United States of America that makes it easier to breed tolerance all through the nation. A nation where people from different cultures and different corners of the world live together and exist together is a nation that is bound to be highly tolerant. The American people have gotten to understand each other and appreciate their differences. It is those differences that shape the unique existence of the American society.

The diversity in America is strengthened by laws that appreciate the uniqueness of the American people, laws that open the nation up for individuality and personal freedoms. People are allowed to practice their religions and embrace their culture without having to live in fear of draconian legislation that would seek to punish them for who they are. The mere existence of diverse cultures in one setting makes it a little bit easier for Americans to tolerate each other or, better still, grow a particular fondness for each other's uniqueness.

Cultural Adaptation and Overcoming Language Barriers

When you first move to a new place, you are without a doubt going to find yourself trying to fit in because you will be feeling out of place. That is a familiar feeling. Almost every immigrant experiences this when they move to America. However, that feeling does not determine your ability to adapt to the new setting, settle, and thrive. Your ability to adapt to the culture and overcome the language barrier, should there be any, is what will propel your success. The following are some of the extraordinarily simple ways you can achieve such a feat:

- **Practice and share your cultural traditions**. Do not shy away from your culture even when you are in profoundly new and challenging setting. Cook the traditional meal and share it with others. Practice your religion and keep embracing your religious beliefs, and without a doubt, you will be able to adjust to the new setting without abandoning who you are. The most important part of this process is sharing your culture and showcasing its amazingly interesting.

- **Create connections with others**. The best way to create connections when you are in a new place is to integrate yourself into the community. Participate in whatever activity the community is engaging in. If the have events, then participate in them, and in the process you get to interact. Interaction is the best way to start connection or bond.

- **Learn English**. English is the most used language in the United States. If you do not know English, then you should learn it so that you can communicate with others.

Chapter 3

Chapter 3

The Importance of English Proficiency

Because English is America's most widely used language, yo need to become proficient. Virtually everything is done in Englis The advertisements are in English, and most businesses operate i English. Even job opportunities are advertised in English. So, th importance of English proficiency cannot be ignored. In essenc being able to communicate well in English will open doors an opportunities. English proficiency makes it easier to communicat with others and interact.

How Mastering English Opens Opportunities in the US

To explain the beauty and importance of English master concerning access to opportunities in the US, let me place befor you a scenario. Mario and Philomena are both immigrants. Mari took the initiative to learn and master English to fit into America society. Philomena did not. When Philomena got to America, sh started looking for jobs. However, all meaningful jobs require certain level of English mastery. She had trouble finding work Meanwhile, Mario completed his English classes and becam fluent. He has been listed as multilingual on job search sites Employers reach out to him, and sometimes, he gets invitations t act as a Spanish interpreter because Spanish is his first language.

Opportunities are open for those who can communicate well. The best way to effectively communicate with almost everyone in America is to be a good English speaker. Effective communication is a skill that every meaningful employer requires. You are not going to be an effective communicator if you can't communicate in the language of the American majority. Master the English language and let it keep those doors open for you.

Resources and Tips for Learning English Efficiently

The beautiful thing about learning a language—be it English or any other language—is that you can have fun while doing it. How do you efficiently learn English and have fun while doing it? The following are some of the amazingly simple ways (*10 top tips*, ed.):

- **Have a circle of English-speaking friends**. The logic behind this tip is simple. If your friends are fluent English speakers, chances are they will implore you to speak English well. You will have to improve your English language skills to communicate effectively with your friends.

- **Read authentic material**. What do I mean by authentic material? This is content that native English speakers have written. Native speakers usually have the nuances of the English language well covered. In essence, your English can only be as good as the material you read from.

- **Embrace fun ways to learn new vocabulary.** Your mastery of English relies on how rich and diverse your vocabulary is. Individuals with a rich vocabulary find communicating easier even in relatively new settings. This is because they already have a sufficient vocabulary depository.

- **Set realistic learning goals**. Do not be the kind who wants to learn everything all at once. Learning and mastering a new language is a gradual and progressive process. Set attainable learning goals and keep on improving steadily.

In addition, apps like Duolingo help people learn new languages and should not be ignored.

Language Proficiency Helps Improve Life

Adrian Mu, an acquaintance, moved from South Sudan to ew York in 2010. At that point, Adrian's English language skills ere lacking, and he found it difficult to conduct basic ommunication. However, things changed when he enrolled in nguage coaching classes. In six months, Adrian had become ighly proficient in English. He started expressing himself better; e made more friends and job opportunities began opening up for im. There is a certain assured improvement that comes to your fe when your language skills get better.

Chapter 4

Chapter 4

Navigating the American Job Market

The American job market is highly competitive. Sometimes, takes more than being good to get what you want. At some point, or you to be recognized and seen as fit for a certain position, you ust be excellent. The standard is even higher when you are an nmigrant. Even though America is the land of equal pportunities, its job market is riddled with occupational biases. or example, certain groups of immigrants are highly employable nd preferable in certain job positions. Think about how most IT obs are looked upon as jobs for Asians.

However, the beauty of this way of doing things is that there always recourse. There are so many ways to navigate the merican job market and make something out of it.

The Job Market and Employment Opportunities for Immigrants

As explained earlier, even though occupational bias exist there are so many job opportunities for immigrants. These ar opportunities designed to attract skilled immigrants to fill in th gaps that citizens could not fill. In a way, America, among a nations, highly benefits from the skills provided by immigrant: Some of the opportunities that immigrants in America may acces are as follows:

The Health-Care Sector

Immigrants come to America with diverse skills, includin healthcare skills. America is a nation that acknowledges th contribution of immigrants to the healthcare sector. As such, ther are readily available opportunities for immigrants, ranging fron medical doctors to nurse aids. Immigrants in this sector brin: professionalism and a touch of empathy. This appealin: combination makes it even easier for such opportunities to b opened for more immigrants.

The Information Technology Sector

This sector fuels innovation and technological change not only in America but also in any organized society. Most immigrants who come to America already possess sufficient skills to seek employment in the sector effectively. It is one of those sectors where immigrants have maintained a high level of competency, making them the priority during the hiring process.

Education and Teaching

There is no doubt that immigrant teachers come from diverse backgrounds and that their diversity comes in handy when it comes to practicing their craft as teachers. They present a diverse range of teaching methodologies that, when adopted and embraced, are tailored to meet each student's specific intellectual or learning requirements. They make the process of instilling academic concepts in the minds of learners much easier and more memorable.

Resume Writing, Interview Preparation, and Job Search Opportunities

A resume tells your professional story without favor or bias. It showcases to the professional world precisely who you are, your achievements, and what you can be expected to achieve shortly. Therefore, preparing a resume must be done with sufficient care and a view toward protecting your professional interests. A good resume should clearly tell your professional story and express your desired professional achievements. The resume opens you up to the hiring world and subsequently leads to your employment.

When it comes to interview preparation, it all depends on what kind of position and organization or institution you would be interviewing for. However, one thing remains constant in all interviews: you must be confident in yourself. Almost every single question in an interview is to test your mastery of the position or field you are interviewing for. Secondly, they test your confidence. The truth is that confidence is a significant trait in all successful individuals. It is essential to research the organization or institution you intend to interview for so that you have in-depth knowledge of their core values and organizational objectives. Even more important is to ensure you align the organization's objective with your objective and ensure your skill set is what they require.

How do you search for job opportunities? That is simple. The best way to find job opportunities is through print and social media advertisements. Sometimes, you may want to visit organizational or institutional websites because that is where you may learn everything that the organization requires. These sites also help ensure the legitimacy of advertisements you may have seen elsewhere.

Understanding Workers and Workplace Culture in the US

The leadership and management of a specific organization or institution majorly influence the workplace culture in America. Management is responsible for formulating and implementing work policies, which inspire and shape the work culture. Various institutions have differing takes on matters like dress code, working hours, and whether you are to work remotely, both remotely and onsite, or just onsite.

However, some of these aspects rely on the labor code of the specific state. You must understand the work culture of the organization you work for so that you may have a seamless and comfortable experience. Perhaps during interviews for jobs, you can ask questions and seek clarification about those issues.

Chapter 5

Chapter 5

Legal and Financial Foundations

As with every process that takes place when moving to a new country in search of opportunities, there are always legal and financial questions. Specific legal and financial standards are in place to ensure your suitability to immigrate to the US.

Visas and Green Cards

To permanently relocate to the US, you need to obtain a green card. The green card sets you up for permanent residency and subsequent citizenship. Sometimes, the process of obtaining green card is somewhat tedious and discouraging, but those who endure get to harvest the fruits. It is important to note that obtaining a green card involves an application and a separate interview process, and those may come at a fee. Paying the fee does not guarantee that you'll get the green card.

A visa is required for short-term visits and stays in the US. When you apply for a visa, be sure you apply for one that is tailored to your objective in the US. For example, if you are going to work, a work visa is appropriate. If you intend to go to school, you need a study visa. Collaborating with the organization you will be working with to support you through the process is always important. Visa applications also require a non-refundable fee.

Understanding the American Tax System and Fulfilling Tax Obligations

The American tax system largely relies on your residenc status. There is no difference in tax obligation between permane residents and citizens. For citizens and residents, the tax is base on your worldwide income, whereas for non-residents, it is base on income accrued in America. An immigrant with a green card considered a lawful permanent resident and is categorized as U.S. tax resident for taxation purposes. The body responsible fc taxation is the IRS (Internal Revenue Service), and it provides a the necessary tax information on its website.

Basic Financial Literacy: Banking Credit Systems an Managing Finances

Some of the critical aspects of financial literacy includ budgeting, saving, debt management, a good credit score, an retirement planning. Budgeting helps you minimize you expenditures and spend responsibly. Operating on a budget is lik having a set of rules constantly reminding you not to break then You're more likely to be strict about what you spend when yo have a budget than when you don't.

Savings are a fundamental part of an immigrant's life. Most of the success of well-to-do immigrants originates from whatever savings they were able to make during their employment or working days. These savings are eventually used to make investments or acquire significant assets. So, savings are a fundamental part of an immigrant's financial journey.

It is also essential to manage your debts as an immigrant. Going into huge debts, you may be unable to repay could jeopardize your future. Maintaining a good credit score and not going into debt is vital. As you get financially better off, remember to invest for your retirement or have a plan to save for it.

Absolutely, you can use the text provided as a template for asking for reviews in your book. However, you may want to adapt it slightly to fit the tone and style of your book. Here's a modified version you could consider:

I hope you've been enjoying "American Dreamer:
An Immigrant's Roadmap to Success in the USA" so far! I'm writing to ask for your help in spreading the word about this book.

If you've found the book helpful and inspiring, would you consider leaving a review? Your feedback can make big difference in helping other immigrants find the guidance they need to thrive in the USA.

Here are some things you might want to mention in your review:
- How has the book helped you or someone you know to navigate life in the USA?
- Your favorite tips, stories, or activities from the book
- Why would you recommend the book to other immigrants?

Thank you so much for your support! Your reviews mean the world to me and other immigrants on their own journey to success.

Happy reading and keep dreaming big.

Choyo Gomex

Chapter 6

Chapter 6

The Path to Education and Professional Development

Before I take you through this chapter on accessing academic opportunities in the American education system, let me tell you story that shows one American immigrant's academic journey.

Choyo Gomex, whose story we told at the beginning of the book after being deported six times, knew deep inside that another deportation could follow at any time. And that if he was deported back to Mexico, it could be for good; then, all his strife would have been for nothing.

He would return to his village and become a farmer like everyone he had grown up with. That was not acceptable, and it was not going to happen. To avoid that, he had to evolve. He knew he had to level up. He needed an upgraded version of himself.

He realized his only way out was education. He needed to educate himself, and everything changed once he made that decision. He figured that with an American college degree and the ability to speak English, he would have other options, and he wouldn't need to be a farmer in his village anymore.

With the help of his mentor, Mr. Earl Nightingale, he enrolled and attended Pepperdine University in Malibu, California, and graduated in 1986, still undocumented.

Mind you, he was a husband, a father, an employee, and a student all at once. He had to cater to his family in the US and Mexico. A degree that was supposed to take four years to complete took him 12 amazingly hard years to finish. With perseverance and a never-give-up attitude, he finally did it!

Choyo left home for work at six a.m. and worked from eight to five; after work, he had to hurry to school. Classes began at six p.m. Already exhausted, he had to study from six p.m. to ten p.m. most days. He had a very rigorous schedule, but he would stop at nothing in the pursuit of his dream. He had classes every weekday, and on weekends, he had a ton of homework and no time to sleep.

Even though it was very tough, and many times he wanted to quit because he felt overwhelmed to the point of tears, deep down inside, he knew that this was the price he had to pay to succeed in life and maybe stay in America.

He was willing to do almost anything, to pay any price, to stay in the United States. Twelve years later, after many sleeples nights, with tears of joy, on August 2, 1986, he graduated from Pepperdine University. After that, his life took a 180-degree turn for the better, and finally, his childhood dream became a reality. He is now very happily living the American dream.

The American PIE

P.I.E. stands for **P**reparation, **I**nformation, and **E**ducation.

When you prepare, inform, and educate yourself, you'll be surprised how "lucky" you'll become and how much easier life can be. In any case, ignorance is much more expensive than the price of education.

If you don't consciously decide to pay the price of success, you are deciding to pay the price of failure by default. An educated mind can recognize and create opportunities. Education is the greatest weapon in humanity's arsenal for survival.

College education is good, and nowadays, with all the technology available to us, educating yourself is a lot easier than it used to be. Even with a college degree, continuing to learn is an indispensable part of personal and professional development.

It empowers individuals, provides access to limitless knowledge, fosters lifelong learning, leads to personal fulfillment, enhances career prospects, and contributes positively to society. In a world where change is the only constant, self-education is a beacon of adaptability, resilience, and continuous growth. Here are some options to educate yourself.

Educational Opportunities from Community Colleges to Universities

Community colleges present diverse opportunities for their students for a low price. You can take courses as complex as radiology, geographic systems, and others at these colleges. The upside of community colleges is that they provide a convenient environment, especially for immigrants who are just starting because the fees are manageable, the classes are small, and the lecturers provide hands-on assistance.

Because of this, most immigrants and international students now prefer to start their academic journeys in America at a community college while they ready their finances and decide on more prominent universities. The role that community colleges play in the development of the lives of immigrants cannot be undervalued.

The importance of universities cannot be ignored, either. Universities have a broader scope and better prospects. They open you up to a diverse range of academic and professional opportunities. While you may start in a community college, working your way to a university is advisable.

ontinuous Learning and Skill Development

The world is in an accelerator mode as far as change is concerned. The required skill sets for specific job opportunities are constantly changing. You must keep improving your skill set and knowledge to meet industry changes. New courses are being introduced to meet the required expertise for the magnificent and novel innovations that are now a part of our daily lives.

True wisdom is acknowledging the change around you and working to mitigate its impact, or at the very least, adapt to the change whenever necessary.

Scholarships, Grants, and Financial Aid Options

A diverse range of scholarship and grant provisions i available for immigrants. These scholarships, grants, and financia aid plans are explicitly designed to help immigrants reach thei academic and professional goals. Some of the readily availabl scholarships include The Bald Eagle Scholarship, the Yolanda an Sam Shuster Scholarship, the Minority Women in LA Scholarship, and many others.

Community colleges and universities also have grants t support their students, which are readily available to immigran students. These are designed to ensure that lack of finances doe not become a permanent obstacle in the academic and professiona journeys of brilliant and determined individuals, at least not i America. The creation of DACA by President Obama in 201 made it possible for undocumented immigrants to enjoy an access an education. Such are the milestones of the great America

Chapter 7

Chapter 7

Entrepreneurship and Starting a Business

Starting a business has, over time, become a convenient way to attain financial stability for immigrants who desire to be their own bosses and make money for themselves. The thing about business and entrepreneurship is that you have to be willing to start. It does not matter how, where, or when. The only thing that matters at the very beginning is your willingness to start. This is not a wild notion or some claim made without evidence. It is something that has been proven by the world's most outstanding entrepreneurs, including Bill Gates, who started Microsoft in a garage, and Mark Zuckerberg, who perfected the idea of Facebook in a dorm room at Harvard.

How Immigrants Can Start Their Businesses in the US

Starting a business as an immigrant in the United States of America is simple. These are the steps you need to take:

- **Settle on a business structure**. Choose the kind of business you want to engage in. Is it a small business? Or are you diving into the large-scale corporate world? After you have decided on the type of business, you will have a clear picture of how you want your business to be structured.

- **Choose where you want to operate your business**. This is the point where you determine which U.S. state best accommodates your business. To make the right decision, you can do a brief background check on how similar businesses have fared before or how they are faring currently.

- **Obtain a registered agent**. A registered agent will help you go through the process of registering and lawfully establishing your business. They are familiar with the procedures and requirements for setting up a business.

- **Obtain a Tax Identification Number**. The Tax Identification Number will be linked to your business for tax deductions and other tax compliance requirements. The TIN is acquired through an application to the IRS that can be made through an online portal on the IRS website.

- **Set up a business account**. Setting up a business account also serves the purpose of compliance with various authorities and governmental requirements. The business account will be linked to your business for all purposes. This account is maintained for the purpose of filing documents with different authorities and relaying the necessary information about your business to the authorities.

- **Maintain business compliance**. Learn and follow the state requirements for your business, as well as any new regulations that may be implemented periodically.

As you can see, owning a business in the US is not complicated. It is doable and extremely simple. The only thing you must gather is capital to get started.

Success Stories of Immigrant Entrepreneurs

In addition to the success stories we already covered in the book's introductory part, let us look at perhaps the most famous example of an immigrant success story: Elon Musk. Born in South Africa, Musk moved to the US in 1990 with a vision to start the most innovative ventures of all time-space exploration and renewable energy. His immigrant status did not stop him. He had a vision and a mission, and that was all that mattered. Elon Musk now runs Tesla, the largest manufacturer of electric cars, and SpaceX, the most innovative and cost-effective space exploration company. You can choose to go as big as Elon Musk did, or you can choose a small venture. The business world is yours to conquer.

Legal and Practical Aspects of Entrepreneurship in America

In all situations in the modern world, you must consider the law. Being an entrepreneur without understanding the laws that regulate your business would be a failure on your part. When it comes to entrepreneurship, the most important laws are property laws, business laws, and tax laws. These provide the guiding principles and ethical limitations of business enterprises and their owners. The laws, or statutes, vary from state to state so you must understand the laws of the specific state where you run your business.

Once your enterprise has been created, the practical aspects of entrepreneurship include managing, assessing, and sustaining the business. This work is hands-on and requires a certain sense of astuteness. When done well, the daily running of your business becomes simple and smooth. So, if possible, it's a good idea to learn how to perform this work flawlessly.

Chapter 8

Chapter 8

Building a Community and Networking

We all exist in some sort of ecosystem where we rely on each other. This is where having a network of people becomes handy and you must build that network or community. There are many instances when working together or having a support system makes everything extremely easy.

Building a Social and Professional Network

The impact of having a social and professional network as you build yourself up, or even after you reach the top, cannot be understated. Social and professional networks provide you with connections that improve all aspects of your life. It is these networks that help you out in times of trouble, the same networks that will open you up for opportunities. Sometimes, belonging to a social network may provide better opportunities than your academic credentials or professional life. It is often said that you ought to have friends who will mention your name in a room full of opportunities. Social and professional networks are those friends, or at the very least, they will provide one friend who can do that for you.

Community Organizations and Immigrant Support Groups

Community organizations and immigrant support groups are like your family, even if they are not your blood relatives. In the case of immigrant support groups, their importance is quite simple. Because the members are immigrants, it's easier for them to understand the challenges you may be facing and provide support. Chances are they have encountered the same challenges, and they know precisely how to go about resolving them.

The same applies to community organizations. You live in the same locality, so you likely face the same challenges. Belonging to and engaging with community organizations is extremely important. They provide an avenue for interaction and help you develop meaningful relations with other community members.

Leveraging Social Media and Professional Platforms for Networking

Social media and professional platforms are awesome avenues for networking. They are capable of reaching a wider audience as well as being able to reach specific groups of individuals. In addition, social media makes work easier for everyone. You can reach almost anyone you want to reach through a simple post or a comment. Keep the following in mind when using social media and professional platforms to enhance your networking experience:

- **Engage your followers**. Running a dormant social media or professional account cannot help you network no matter how many followers you may have. However, the moment you start engaging your followers through live chats and posts, you open a channel for interaction that leads to the expansion of your network.

- **Optimize your content for each platform**. Create content designed for each platform that you use. Certain content may be appropriate for Instagram and yet be inappropriate for LinkedIn. It is important to determine which content fits which platform because the users on one platform may be different from those on another platform.

- **Research and learn about your audience**. You have to know who your audience is on different platforms. This helps you know which content is appealing to them and which one is not. Non-appealing content will only push your network away from you, defeating the very objective of uploading the content in the first place.

Chapter 9

Chapter 9

Overcoming Challenges and Resilience

Challenges are part and parcel of life. As such, it take resilience to deal with them. Being an immigrant is hard. I face deportation several times, and that was my challenge as a immigrant. Ultimately, it was a challenge I conquered, and prevailed. The following are some of the challenges tha immigrants face, together with strategies to overcome them:

- securing a job

- finding housing

- figuring out transportation

- overcoming communication barriers

Securing a job is perhaps the most common challenge faced by immigrants in the early days of arrival in the US. The mos viable options for this challenge include better networking, joining community groups, and sometimes starting as a volunteer to showcase skills.

To communicate better, the most common solution is to learn
the English language. You can learn English from friends, enroll
in an English class, or even take tutorials from YouTube.

On the part of the housing, community groups can help you
seek assistance with housing and keep an eye on advertisements
for available accommodations. Regarding transportation, you can
always look up the nearest public transportation system.

Stories of Resilience and Success Amid Adversity

There are so many stories of immigrants who have faced
difficult times and, in the end, thrived. These people remind us
that life is full of ups and downs, but remaining down is
unacceptable. Such people have thrived in the face of adversity.
They woke during the bad days and kept going, heads held high,
and minds focused on a singular objective: to do better for
themselves and their loved ones.

One such story is that of another acquaintance, Rotich, a engineering student who left Kenya in search of greener pasture and the pursuit of the American dream. On arrival in America things did not go well for him. He lost all his money and had n way to buy food or access accommodations. His hopes of findin a decent job deteriorated, and he ended up being helpless an begging on the streets of New York. However, one day, Rotic woke up to a surprise visitor; a local non-governmenta organization had taken the initiative to offer somewhat meaningfu jobs for the homeless. He put in his hard work and started gainin recognition among the founders of the organization.

One year after the fact, his life changed for the better. He nov lives in New York and still works at the organization that save his life.

Balancing Cultural Identity with Assimilation

People are who they are, and deep down, they have specific aspects that keep them unique from others. Cultural identity is one such aspect. You do not have to abandon who you are; instead, you can fight for who you are. If you allow yourself to be fully assimilated and, in return, abandon your culture, then you have abandoned yourself, the very fiber of your being.

Remember that even as you fit into a new environment, you ought to be able to balance between identity and the urge to fit in. Fitting in is essential sometimes, but it should not be at the expense of losing yourself.

Chapter 10

Chapter 10

The Undocumented

The story of the undocumented American immigrant might be one of struggle, anxiety, and constant dodging. It is also humane and magical. It is not just about people living underground and leading shadowy lives. The story involves love, life, procreation, providence, and prosperity, with the natural love of the universe shining upon them. Like all the inhabitants of the globe, the undocumented American immigrant is driven by the pursuit of a better life, a better future, and sometimes just mere survival.

The lives of two sisters born in Zacatecas, Mexico, show how it is possible to shine a light at the end of the tunnel that entrenches the undocumented American immigrant. Growing up in Mexico, the twins had it rough and complicated. Being young female children in a society that idolized male bravado did not make it easier for them.

They had a life riddled with poverty and discomfort i
addition to all the societal plights. Decent meals were scarce, an
so was a sober environment for the growth and development o
children as young and brilliant as they were. Their father ofte
came to America for construction work, and their house had t
accommodate eight of their father's brothers.

The general environment was no longer hospitable for them
and their father had to decide whether to bring them to Americ
undocumented or not. His decision was beyond documentatio
bureaucracy; his kids' future was at stake, and America was hi
only hope. It was more about survival.

In America, the twins grew up mastering the art of concealin
their identity and the true nature of their presence in America
They had to live shadowy lives with extreme care, not to revea
intimate facts about their identity or the lives of their families i
any way.

This was a heavy burden for young children with friends, playmates, and classmates who often exuded humongous curiosity levels. This often made them feel unwanted and unwelcome in a country where they grounded their faith and dreams.

Their story started getting better when they got to junior high school, where their brilliance and academic excellence were undeniable. They eventually graduated as valedictorians at the top of their class. Luckily enough, former President Obama created DACA, or Deferred Action for Childhood Arrivals, in 2012, and their options massively changed. They no longer had to live in fear of being deported to Mexico or having to go to community college, even when they were brilliant enough to go directly to a university. There was not just a ray of hope but rather a whole spectrum of it. They enrolled in Notre Dame University as some of the first undocumented students (O'Shaughnessy, 2015).

Challenges of the Undocumented

The journey of undocumented immigrants in America is fraught with struggles, fears, and challenges that shape their daily lives. The undocumented immigrant community, often fleeing dire circumstances in their homelands, arrives in the United States with the hope of a safer, more prosperous future. Yet, upon arrival, they face an existence shadowed by the constant anxiety of discovery and the very real threat of deportation.

One of the most immediate struggles for undocumented immigrants is the barrier to legal employment. Without the proper authorization to work, many find themselves in low-paying jobs that are often unstable and exploitative.

Employers often take advantage of their status by paying them below minimum wage, subjecting them to unsafe working conditions, or denying them basic labor and human rights. The fear of being reported to immigration authorities binds many to silence, making them invisible victims in a system that benefits from their labor while denying their rights (Villavicencio, 2020).

Undocumented immigrants also grapple with limited access to health care and education. The fear of being identified and possibly deported deters many from seeking medical attention, leading to untreated illnesses and the exacerbation of chronic conditions.

For children of undocumented immigrants, the pursuit of public education is also clouded by uncertainty. Although public schools in the US do not require proof of citizenship, the journey beyond high school is beset with hurdles, from the inaccessibility of financial aid to the ever-looming threat that their family might be torn apart by immigration enforcement at any moment.

The psychological toll of living undocumented cannot be overstated. The constant stress and anxiety can lead to a host of mental health issues, including depression and post-traumatic stress disorder. The fear of separation from family members who may be deported—or who may have been left behind in their country of origin—hangs heavy on the hearts of undocumented immigrants (Villavicencio, 2020).

The community lives with the paradox of striving to build a better life in the shadows, knowing that the foundations of that life could crumble at any instant. They go to work in the morning, not knowing if they will see their family that evening.

On top of that, the challenge of integration into American society is compounded by the political and social climate. Undocumented immigrants often face discrimination and xenophobia, which can manifest in racial profiling, hate crimes, or simply the everyday indignities of being treated as second-class citizens, as less than human. The divisive political rhetoric surrounding immigration further alienates this community, reinforcing the notion that they are unwanted intruders rather than individuals seeking refuge and opportunity.

In the face of these adversities, undocumented immigrants display remarkable resilience. They establish close-knit communities that provide mutual support and advocacy. They find innovative ways to contribute to the economy, enrich the nation's cultural tapestry, and advocate for legal reforms. They live with the hope that America will one day recognize their invaluable contributions and afford them the dignity and security they deserve.

Undocumented immigrants' journey in America is a testament to human endurance and the unyielding desire for a better life. It is a narrative that challenges the conscience of the nation, calling into question the ideals of freedom and justice that America purports to uphold. As a society, there is a moral imperative to address these struggles, to alleviate these fears, and to overcome these challenges—not only for the undocumented community but for the soul of America itself.

Community and Support

Despite the inevitable challenges, the undocumented community is not devoid of beautiful stories—stories of love, solidarity, and immense support. Even amid struggles and evident hardships, the community comes together to support and uphold each other. When one is in need, they come together to raise funds, hire lawyers, and, in many other ways, be their brothers' keepers.

In addition to their communal organizations and initiatives to support each other when in need, other groups also pitch in to help. In California, various higher education institutions, including universities like Los Angeles City College, Sacramento City College, and many others, have formulated ways to support those students who are undocumented or have no legal status.

This is a community that pushes beyond the set limits to achieve their goals and dreams, and those dreams are the building blocks of the collective American dream. It does no harm to empathize, support, show love, and uplift each other. We all have a shared objective to improve our lives, be it immigrants, the undocumented, legal citizens, or even foreigners.

Conclusion

The journey from your homeland to a new land to start a new life or pursue a dream could be difficult. However, ultimately, it is worthwhile to commit yourself to your goals and aspirations. Your focus ought to be on the path that you have chosen. Let the focus light the way and propel you toward greater things.

The chapters in this book have highlighted the journey of an immigrant in the US in a way that is easier to understand. The strategies provided are easy to implement, so the book is a simplified manual for your journey as an immigrant. The chapters are full of examples that you can quickly identify with and can remind you that many have taken the journey you are on, and they have excelled. There is no reason why you should be an exception. May the enduring spirit of the ever-conquering immigrant light your path.

As the pages of *American Dreamer: A Tale of Beginnings and Hopes* come to a close, we are reminded of the unfolding poignant journey. This story, woven with dreams, struggles, and the relentless pursuit of a better life, resonates deeply with the core of the human spirit.

In the twilight of our tale, we find our protagonist, who started as a hopeful dreamer, standing at the precipice of his realized dreams. His journey, marked by both triumphs and tribulations, mirrors the quintessential American dream—a testament to the power of resilience, hope, and unwavering determination.

A sense of overwhelming gratitude and fulfillment washed over him as he gazes upon the fruits of his labor. The journey was arduous, filled with moments of doubt and despair, but it was those very challenges that carved out the strength and wisdom he now possesses. His story is not just one of success but of transformation—a metamorphosis from a dreamer into a doer, a seeker into a finder, and a hopeful into an achiever.

This tale, though deeply personal, echoes the universal longing for a better life in every individual's heart. It serves as a poignant reminder that pursuing the American dream, with all its hurdles and uncertainties, is a journey worth taking. It is a narrative that inspires, urging each of us to hold onto our dreams, face our fears with courage, and never lose sight of life's endless possibilities.

As the sun sets on our story, we leave our protagonist not at an end but at the beginning of a new chapter. His journey reminds us that every dream, no matter how distant, is within reach if pursued with passion and perseverance. *American Dreamer: A Tale of Beginnings and Hopes* is more than a story; it's a beacon of inspiration for dreamers everywhere who dare to reach for the stars and carve their path in the pursuit of happiness and fulfillment.

In this heartfelt conclusion, we are not saying goodbye. We are standing witness to the birth of a new dream, a new journey. As readers, we are left with a renewed sense of hope and a reminder that the American dream, in its many forms, is alive and thriving in the hearts of those who dare to dream.

The journey from your homeland to a new land to start a new life or pursue a dream is a difficult one. However, in the end, it is worthwhile if you commit yourself to your goals and aspirations. Your focus ought to be on the path that you have chosen. Let the focus light the way and propel you toward greater things.

See you at the top, my fellow traveler,

Choyo Gomex

I hope you've been enjoying "American Dreamer: An Immigrant's Roadmap to Success in the USA" so far! I'm writing to ask for your help in spreading the word about this book.

If you've found the book helpful and inspiring, would you consider leaving a review? Your feedback can make a big difference in helping other immigrants find the guidance they need to thrive in the USA.

Here are some things you might want to mention in your review:

- How the book has helped you or someone you know to navigate life in the USA

- Your favorite tips, stories, or activities from the book

- Why would you recommend the book to other immigrants?

Thank you so much for your support! Your reviews mean the world to me and to other immigrants who are on their own journey to success.

Happy reading and keep dreaming big!

Choyo Gomex

References

Jordan, M. (2023, March 13). Many undocumented immigrants are departing after decades in the U.S. *The New York Times*. www.nytimes.com/2023/03/01/us/undocumented-immigrants-exodus-us.html

O'Shaughnessy, B. (2015). *Shattering the silence: Undocumented twins share their story*. University of Notre Dame. https://www.nd.edu/stories/shattering-the-silence

Tax Information and Responsibilities for New Immigrants to the United States. (2024, February 6). Internal Revenue Service. www.irs.gov/individuals/international-taxpayers/tax-information-and-responsibilities-for-new-immigrants-to-the-united-states

10 Inspiring Stories of Immigrant Entrepreneurs Who Made It Big. (2023, December 12). Faster Capital. fastercapital.com/content/10-Inspiring-Stories-of-Immigrant-Entrepreneurs-Who-Made-It-Big.html#:~:text=industries%20and%20communities

10 Top Tips for Learning English at Home. (n.d.). EF English Live. englishlive.ef.com/en/blog/study-tips/10-top-tips-learning-english-home

U.S. culture: getting to know Americans. (n.d.). University of California San Francisco International Students and Scholars Office. isso.ucsf.edu/us-culture

Villavicencio, K.C. (2020). *The Undocumented Americans*. New York: One World